TALES OF THE HEART

The heart has a voice.

By: Asithandile Gqwaka

MY PAST

I won't tell you about my past.
But I will tell you,
it keeps me awake at night.
My heart pounds while my brain
gets filled with gloomy prospects.
Meanwhile the fume of my burning heart
suffocates my lungs.

I won't take you back to my past,
 But I will give you a glance.
at how dim my life was from all cardinal
directions,
A peek at how my heart was bailing out on me,
just like everyone else.
A glance at how every, "I promise".
Every" I love you" is now questioned.
Because then, they turned to empty promises
and meaningless syllables.

However, I'm not one to hang on to the past.

So, I'd rather journey you through my current
life.
Promises no longer have weight in my heart,
so even when they're broken, they won't leave
a vacuum that'll be filled with tears.

Now every morning I drink at least one glass of
self-reliance to get me through the day.
The week.
The months.
 The years.

I won't bore you about my past.
But I will tell you that I am, because she was.

I'M OKAY

Every time they ask, "How are you?"
I always smile and say, "I'm okay".
And when they ask, "how has life been?"
I say, "It's been great".
But that is all a lie.

When I say, "I'm okay", my heart sheds blood.
While my eyes suppress tears.
My brain fights with my mouth on whether I
should open and tell them:
How sleepless I get at night,
How wet my one pillow gets,
while my other console my body.

But I end up saying "I'm okay".
Because they won't get it.
They will never understand how my nightmares
haunt me,
How my brain plays with me:
Selling me fake horrifying future events.

So, I choose to say, "I'm okay".

Because if not, they'll think I'm crazy.

UNCHAIN MY HEART

I wish deleting you in my brain was as easy as
it is on the phone.
I wish my being free of your memories was just
a button away.
That with just one click, your existence in my
brain would vanish.

You are stuck in my hippocampus: a parasite.
You are sucking on my joy.
You are hanging onto my heart like jewellery.

I am trying to get over you,
But as I take one step forward, a memory of
you blows me 10 steps back.

This is no longer healthy.
This is not love.
I know I should be moving on from you,
Finding myself outside of you,

But the future I created in my head includes
You.

Before you I was a free spirit, no attachment
issues.
After you, my heart is chained to yours, all it
wants is to be loved and taken care of.
But all you're doing is torture it.
You have no reason to make it suffer, but
you're doing it.

It might not have a voice,
But it does have feelings.
Please, unchain my heart,
Rescue it from this misery!

LOST AT SEA

I hate myself for absorbing your ill-treatment.
But I'm wise enough now to know that it
continued because I let it.
I hate myself for loving you so much that I
forgot to love myself.

Settling for the bare minimum and not knowing
my worth.
For giving you everything on a silver platter,
While you made my life a living hell,
Treating me like trash.
So, I hate myself, for not knowing when it was
time to hit the road, time to give up on a person
who wasn't even trying to be with me.

I tried so much to look for the good inside you,
that I was almost certain is in there.
Poured my all in you so you would do the
same.

I lost my dignity in the process.
I lost myself in the process.
I forgot to love myself in the process.
Now I'm lost at sea.
Trying to find myself, who I was, before you
devoured my soul.

I loved you so much that I turned a blind eye
when your actions were telling me that you
didn't value me.
I guess I wanted you so bad, that I refused to
acknowledge that you didn't want me.

Clearly, I hated myself.
I hated myself so much that I would beg for
your attention.
So much that I worshiped you.

I came to a decision that you were an
emotionally unavailable person.
That was me making excuses for you.

Because I didn't want to believe that you didn't want me.

It is now I realize I eventually had to draw a line.

And love me.

BUT TO YOU

To me our relationship was a treasure.
One I wouldn't trade for anything.
I invested in us: I could see my dream's
reflection in us.
When counting my blessings I counted it twice.
I wanted to cater to your every need,
I wanted you to be happy.

But to you I was a ladder to greater heights.
All you did was take and take and take.
Now that I think about it, no, you never loved
me.
You loved what I had to offer.
I wasn't a fool for putting your needs before
mine, I was in love.

I laid my worth near the riverbank so I could
hold on to you.
I let go of who I was, my beliefs, to please you.
I imprisoned my femininity, so you'd love me.

I chose you, over me.

I continued to betray myself, allowing you to
make me your second best,
Even after realizing you'd never love me as
much as you loved her.

Every time they ask me why I love you so
much, I'd scratch my head, mumble.
Because all you were, was a burden.
You had absolutely nothing to offer.
All you did was take and take and take.

You didn't deserve me.
I could've left found someone better.
But I chose to stay, make you better.
Clearly you weren't worthy of that,
nor me.

I FORGAVE

He was my first love.
He introduced love to me.
He stamped an image in my mind of what love
is.
He defined love for me.
And his definition is all that I knew.
He convinced me that I must fight for love.
That love comes with a lot of complications.
That Love is painful.

So that was my love.
Sleepless nights, wetting my pillow,
Having to constantly beg him to treat me right.
Writing long paragraphs pouring my heart out
to him.
And he'd read them with a glance of an eye: no
emotion.
Tossing and turning in my bed trying to find
reasons why he is hurting me like this.

That was the love he introduced to me.
A love that I got used to and allowed.

Being the one who caters to his needs, him
taking a back seat while I put in all the effort.
Being asked to not label our relationship
because titles come with entitlement.

Situationships were all that I knew.
Toxic situationships where I was a
convenience.
Yet I was convinced that, that's what love is.
Because I knew none other than that.

The only love I knew was the one where I put
his needs before mine.
Where I loved him more than I love myself.

A love that comes with a lot of disrespect that I
had to forgive.
And I forgave and I forgave, and I forgave:

Times when he would not reply to my texts
making me feel like I'm annoying,
And I forgave when he gave other girls more
attention than me, posting them on his socials,
while I had to understand that our relationship
was private.

And I forgave when he made me feel like I'm
not beautiful enough to be shown to the world,
And I forgave when he would make me feel like
I'm forcing myself unto him because I was
begging for him to notice me.
And I forgave when he never took me out on a
date: making me feel like I'm not worth a
penny.

And I forgave when he gave his new girl all that
I ever asked for and loved her loudly and
proudly.
Unlike me was worth to be shown to the world.
And I forgave when he only reached out to me
when he needed help and I delivered.

But now I'm stuck here unable to forgive
myself.
For allowing him to treat me like trash.
Staying despite knowing that I deserved better.

Now I'm stuck here, unable to forgive and
forgive and forgive myself,
 For being naive thinking, I would teach him
how to love me.
But for him I forgave, and I forgave, and I
forgave,
Because in my eyes forgiving was love,
And that love is all that I was used to.

For being naive thinking, I would teach him
how to love me.
But for him I forgave, and I forgave, and I
forgave,
Because in my eyes forgiving was love,
And that love is all that I was used to.

TELL ME HOW TO MOVE ON

I tried to convince myself that I was over you.
That my unconditional love for you has faded.
I tried to convince myself: I have healed from
you,
Whenever I hear your name, it'll no longer put
a smile on my face.
Nor make my heartbeat faster.

Then triggers sent me back to square one.
The smallest things that remind me of you
resurfaced all the moments that made me fall
in love with you.
Memories of you rejuvenate my love for you.

Clearly, I haven't healed.
No, I haven't forgotten you at all.

TEACH ME HOW TO BE ENOUGH

All I ever wanted was to show you love.
That you would find a home. In me.
Like a hen shielding its chicks, I'd provide
refuge for your heart.
A safe space where you would unload your
burdens.
With tenderness I would dress your wounds.

But you chose her.
You wanted her.
Teach me how to be like her.
Teach me how to be just like her:
Win your heart without trying.
She didn't have to finch to win you.
I crossed oceans to get your approval.
Yet you didn't hesitate to leave me for her.

So, tell me what to do to be enough for you.
To be what you want and who you want.
Because you are what I want and need.

I still want to gaze into your eyes and see an
image of my future.
To make your chest my forever resting place.
To wear you like coat.
I want you.
Only you.

BIGGEST LIE I EVER TOLD MYSELF

At first, you were everything I wanted.
For you, I would've walked barefoot on a sand
full of thorns.
That's how fond of you I was.
You were my heart's greatest desire.

Then like a wolf you devoured my life.
Like a creature from hell,
You disheartened my soul.

Yet you continued to be happy,
Despite hurting me.
I thought I hated you for that.
I thought hearing your name would make me
shiver.

But my heart is still tender attached to you.
And for that I am disgusted in myself.
I tried so much to fight my feelings.

So much that I would convince myself that I hated you.
But that was the biggest lie I ever told myself.

Because hearing your name still puts a smile on my face, butterflies in my stomach and solace in my heart.
So, no. I don't hate you at all.

TO MY NEXT LOVE

I hope that he makes me feel alive.
That his reliance restores the spirit of trust I
had buried.
I hope that he heals my inner child:
Unloading all I had took on which was not mine
to carry.
I hope that he revives my tender essence.
That I can finally let my guard down,
And let my femininity flourish.

I hope that he feeds my soul.
That his presence calms my nerves.
That he makes me feel wanted. Needed.
I hope that he loves me without condition:
From surface level to the deepest parts of my
soul.

I hope that he becomes my escape from
reality.
That he caters to my feminine needs.

Presents need I didn't know I required.
I hope that he becomes all that I've ever
dreamed of.

I hope that he does to me what knowledge
does to the mind:
Feeds my curiosity.
I hope that he ignites the perfect warmth in my
heart,
That he becomes the highlight of my life.

INFINITE BITTERSWEET LOVE

How do I love someone new,
When every night I dream of you?
How do I let go of us,
When in every love song I devote the lyrics to
you?
How do I move on, while I get turned on by just
a thought of you?

Our love story is a personification of
bittersweet.

Your sweet lips are my comfort zone.
Yet the poisonous words they utter wound me.
Your chest solaces my grief:
Unaware that deep inside your heart she lies.
My heart belongs to you, while yours belongs
to her.

How will I ever forget you,

When you're the rubric I use to measure,
looking for a new person?
None compares to you.

I always imagine how gleeful our reunion would
be.
How perfect our second chance love story
would be.
My heart still desires your touch:
The cause and antidote of my anxiety attacks.

You are the God of my heart,
The creator of my happiness,
Savior of my soul.
Yet today my heart bleeds and my hands
shake because of you.

ABOVE ALL ELSE

Like Jazz your voice gives tranquil pleasure to
my ears.
Like one with a loud bass, it makes the
butterflies in my stomach flip.
Like water your kisses satisfy my quench.
Like sunrise after dawn your smile illuminates
my dark days.

Your hugs are therapy to my soul.

In your eyes I see my dreams reflection,
The answer to my questions.

I am attracted to you in ways I cannot explain.
You make me feel like a kid in a candy store.

You are it. You are my person.

I NOW KNOW WHAT LOVE IS

I knew.
Just by how my lips curl when you stare at me,
How my brows rise when I hear your name.
And how my heart races when I see you.

I knew I was in love when your smile set my
face on fire,
How your kisses became the cure to my
anxiety.

I knew you were the answer to my prayers,
when all I could say in prayer was," Dear God,
Thank you".
With a big smile, I had no other words.
No requests. I had all I needed.

I knew you were my place of comfort:
You reminded me of sunsets and waterfalls.
Whenever I laid in your chest,
I felt at peace, I felt home.

That's how I knew.

Even in my busy schedules mind found time to think of you:

A thought of you rejuvenates my strength.

OUR HONEYMOON PHASE

Take me back to our honeymoon phase, when
all you did was love me.
When all you ever wanted was to take care of
me.
Take me back to when every inch of your body
flirted with me,
From your eyes adoring every part of me to
your legs wrapped around my body.
Because you always wanted me close to you.

Or was this a short-term pleasure?
 Your way of making me fall in love with you,
For you to not even love me,
To waste my time.

Now I'm stuck here,
unable to move on from you.
Unable to forget the times you would treat me
like a baby and kiss every part of my body.

Unable to forget your unconditional love, how
you adored me.
Unable to forget the times you would make
every day of my life Valentine's Day.
You loved me. You enjoyed me.

But now all you do is to make every day of my
life is glimpse of hell.
All you do: is make me regret ever meeting
you.
And I don't know where We went wrong.
All I ever did was love you.

I HAD A DREAM LAST NIGHT

In this dream you turned fairytales into
existence.
You touched my hand; your angelic touch
bandaged the wounds in my hands.
The spark in your veins reached my bleeding
heart: stanched every drop.

In this dream you loved me.
 With every one of your kisses, I felt healed.
With every word that you uttered my soul found
a home.
And in your smile, I found every reason to want
to stay in dream land.

You became my most expensive treasure.

However, when I woke up from this dream,
I still felt every emotion,
 I am still madly in love with you.
So please.

Turn my dreams into reality.

Make my fantasy island my everyday life.

So that me finding real love isn't only a figment

of my imagination.

But the life I get to live every day of my life.

SO, I PRETEND

I pretend like you are not hurting me,
So, I can hang on to you.
Whenever I must repeat myself 2,3 times and
you never seem to listen,
 I adjust and find a reason to accept your
behaviour.
Because leaving you is never an option.

So, I accept your ill-treatment and pretend like
it's not hurting me.
So now I love pretending, Because I love you.

MY EMOTIONS

My emotions are extraordinary.
In overwhelming circumstances, they devour
me.
They are never neutral.

When I am hurt, they suffocate me,
When I'm happy they brighten my days.

My emotions are my greatest strength,
Yet can be my weakness.
When I'm in love I barely sleep,
The butterflies in my stomach get the best of
me,
They make me feel alive.
I lose focus in conversations:
My brain gets filled with fantasies.

Someone help me, I can't control my emotions.
They are splashing all over like a kid's
colouring.

The same emotions are my place of comfort.
Creating fantasies brightens my mood.
Listening to a song and pretending its
dedicated to me, soothes my soul.

My emotions hug me.
They brighten my dark days.
They give me life.
Yet they suffocate me: overthinking past
misfortunes.

Someone help me.
My emotions are consuming me.

YOU ARE A GLIMPSE OF HELL

I want to wake up in the morning and not have
a picture of you as my first thought.
I want to not have you as the last thing on my
mind.
I want to forget you as easily as you forgot me.

But maybe the reason why I'm so hung up on
you: no one makes me feel how you made me
feel.
None have come close to how tingly my
stomach gets when you look deep into my
eyes.

But I no longer want to constantly think of you
every hour of my day,
when you don't even remember that I am a
living person.
I no longer want to have you in my mind
whenever I listen to a love song.

I need to wake up from this dream of thinking
that one day you'll change,
be the man that I need.
That one day you will love me as much as I
love you.

But no matter how much you show me that I
deserve better, I struggle to let you go.

Like a disease you are devouring my life
Like one with no cure, I watch you mercilessly
destroy me,
and my hope of ever believing in love again.
I no longer have it in me to believe someone
who says they love me.

So, thank you.
Thank you for ruining my idea of love,
For showing me that not everyone who says
they love me, mean it.
And thank you so for the wakeup call.

ICE COLD HEART

You are my best friend.
My place of comfort.
But like a bat you secretly live a double life.
You stain my image, ruin my reputation,
Pretending to be my saviour.

Your chest that I relied on as my embrace and
safe place,
To pour my problems,
Now became a poison storage:
Spits venom and bruises my heart.

The coffee we used to drink,
To sweep down my pain,
You now drink with my enemies,
Unfolding my confidential information.

Quarrelled is my soul.
For once, we baked cookies together.
Now you bake my name with my tormenters.

So cold and heartless you are.

So dark and poisonous.

Still, you were my bosom.

My supposed safe place.

IF THIS IS LOVE

You're saying you love me.
Where does this love go,
when I'm lying in the bathroom floor crying
because days have passed without a text from
you.

Where is that love when for the past month
your texts are getting colder and colder,
when the empty spaces in our conversations
are filled with my tears.
When the calls that are not answered leave
questions in my head: whether I still matter.

I search for the love you're saying you have for
me,
I come back empty handed because the truth
is right in front of me.

You no longer want me, no amount of busy
would hinder a person from speaking to
someone they love for days.
Weeks.
Months.
If this is your definition of love, then clearly,
we're not compatible.

Now I'm holding on to the memories of how
you loved me, your silly habits that I loved, you
squeeze into my clothes,
staring at my mouth while I speak.
because you craved for me.

What was the point of making me fall in love
with you, if you will confuse me like this.
For you to not even love me.

I know what love is, I've been loved before.
When you love someone, you make time for
them, value them, prioritize them.

Not make them feel like they're forcing
themselves unto you.

No number of busy schedules can cause you
to go days not talking to the one you love.
Yet again, I do not want any attention from you
that you do not want to give voluntarily.

I do not wish this emotional fatigue even on my
greatest enemy.
From asking to be seen, heard and
understood, begging to be noticed.
to see that I love you.

So, I don't know.

I don't know if continuing to chase you is worth
the heartache,
feeling my heart break into a million pieces.
I wish you knew how much you are breaking
me: forcing me to stop loving you.
when all I want is to love every inch of you.

WITHOUT YOU

I will never forgive you for fetching me from my
peace and making me create a soft spot for
you,
 only for you to destroy me.
Not only did you destroy my mental health, but
you made sure to make me question everyone
who ever said they loved me.
I hanged on to you despite you giving me every
reason to leave.
I continued to love you even when I realized
that loving you was destroying me.
I cared for you more than I cared for myself.

And for that I will never forgive.

I will never forgive You for awakening my love
only for yours to rest peacefully and leave mine
lonely.

I will never forgive you for all those times you would promise to change, and I would fall for your acts.
Because I feared who I would be without you.

But it turns out that without you, I have peace, without you I AM happiness. Without you I love myself.

MY HEART IS TIRED

I no longer have attachment issues.
I no longer feel the need to hold on to people
despite their ill-treatment.
Holding on to people because of how fond of
them I am and my desperation to be loved by
them.
And hoping that one day they will see how
much I want them in my life and eventually
want me in theirs.

I am tired of staying in the hope that I can love
them into loving me.
I have overgrown my desperation of being in
people's lives who make it very clear that they
don't mind not having me in theirs.

Yes, I may still love them,
but I am tired of forcing myself into people's
lives.
My heart is tired and so too is my soul.

YOU HAVE BECOME A STRANGER

I've noticed you changing from using a lot of
heart emojis in every text,
to no emojis at all.
I watched you loving me like crazy, to thinking
that I'm crazy.
From caring about me so much to not feeling
any guilt after hurting me.
Not feeling any remorse when I shed tears due
to your ill-treatment.
To not caring enough to change your ways
when I tell you I don't like a certain trait.

I watched you making a habit of caring about
me only when you feel like it.
It is hard for me to accept that your love for me
is slowly fading,
hard for me to look at you look at me and
feeling nothing.
It is hard for me to accept that the man who
used to love me from surface level,

has now become a stranger.

But I hope that one day I will be realistic with
myself and accept that your change in
behaviour,
is due to your change of heart.

I WILL NEVER BELIEVE IN LOVE AGAIN

It took me a while to understand that no matter
how many times they say they love you and
remind you of how much you mean to them, it
doesn't mean that they truly feel that way.

So, I hope that my next love won't break my
heart,
That he won't be like them and disconnect the
relationship between his mouth and his heart
and brains.

Because of them, today I fear love,
Or maybe it's not love that I fear.
Just the fear that everyone will be just like the
last person who destroyed me.

They ruined my idea of love,
They repainted the image in my mind of what
love looks like,

They twisted and gave me the opposite of the
love I had in my dreams,
They made my fantasies come true but on in
reverse motion.

And because of them, I will never believe in
love again.

I WILL NEVER FORGIVE YOU

I sit in the mirror all day,
wondering what features I can change to be
perfect for you.
I want to hear the words "you are beautiful "and
let them mean something to me.
I want to believe them.
Believe that they describe me.

But how do I believe anyone who says I'm
beautiful,
when the one person who is supposed to
admire all of me treats me like the world's
ugliest person?

How will they ever mean anything to me when
the love of my life still looks at other girls and
makes me feel not enough?

You have created a deep hole in my heart,

A vacuum that used to contain self-security

and self-love.

And for that, I will never forgive you.

BEAUTY IN DISGUISE

Loving people is beautiful,
Being of people is seeable,
Being generous to others is warmly.

That was me.
My heart was so warm that it heated people's
homes and gave them warm smiles in a way
the sun never could.
My hands were wildly open such that they
couldn't keep anything enclosed for their
owner.

Then people started to be, people.
Their betrayal killed my kindness,
Buried it with disappointments.
Now beneath the surface it lies in stash,
My reliance was abused and taken advantage
of,
Like a boomerang it backfired.

Where do good hearted people live in this world full of parasites?

In a world full of vile people who press one's buttons till they explode

Now I choose to be beauty and the beast.

A villain is my recent personal appearance.

Beauty in disguise.

She is my weakness.

Her fragile being is the cause of my internal wounds.

But without her wounding I would still be people's yo-yo.

I AM DONE

I no longer want to be heard,
Nor seen.
I no longer feel the need,
To feel important in people's lives,
Or the desire to be checked up on.

I no longer want any affirmation.
Or approval.

I just want to be left alone.
I want to live in my own world.

Because the last time I heard those words,
I indirectly forced it out of him,
I constantly reminded him to compliment me.
But now that I no longer remind him,
He started doing it voluntarily.
But it's a little too late.
Because I no longer need him to.

I no longer live by his affirmations.

Cause I am done waiting for people,
To tell me my worth, how I look,
And just how important I am.

SHE IS MY BEST FRIEND

She doesn't wear heels.
she doesn't do nails, nor put makeup on.
She doesn't like flowers, necklaces nor
bracelets.
But she is a lady.
She prefers a basket of goodies than a basket
of roses.
She doesn't have curves or a huge ass and
boobs, or none.
But she is a woman, a lady.

Her natural beauty she wears like a crown.
Her curvy legs are a glimpse of paradise,
Her charming smile is warm like a winter coat.
But her hugs are warmer.
She likes hugs, she is cuddly.

Ladies are known to be nurturing.
Euphemism is often their method of avoiding
the truth.

But not my best friend

She is raw.

She is a personification of refined in every way.

She dishes the truth unprocessed.

She is crude, natural is her preference.

She hates perfumes, she smells earthly.

Her natural scent is the most divine scent I've
ever beheld.

Like fresh air my inner organs are fond of her.

My outer organs are just as fond.

The high self-esteem and confidence she
instilled upon me sparkles.

She taught me to not be a prisoner to the
things I cannot change.

She is my rescuer.

She completes me.

She is the final piece to my puzzle.

Yes, she is my best friend, my life partner.

EVERYTHING, EVERY WAY

I find no pleasure hearing him acquainted as
merely an actor.
Where does one begin to give a title that
amounts to the mighty and versatile Mr
Masire?

Rumour says he is a wolf in a sheep's clothing.
Rumour says he might blow my brains to
death.
Sadly, phumlani isn't here to manifest the
hearsay.

In my eyes you are a well-mannered charming
gentleman Mr Dlamini.

But why am I suffocating by just a glance at
you?
Could it be your charming smile taking my
breath away, or is chloroform one of your killing
methods?

Your voice menaces me to give you all I have.
No, you are a villain in a suit Mr Ngonyama.
But your eyes are still inviting me to long for
making your chest my pillow.

Your laughter is therapeutic like a glass of
water.
It turns me on without you even trying.
That is a rare skill you possess Mr Xaluva.
Or could all the breeds of the broad new
brighten be blessed with that ability?

Manifesting on God for your chest to be my
coffin, my internal resting place.

Where do I begin to tell you that I literally want
to live inside you without sounding weird,
Because your smile massages my internal
organs.
When they say suited for each other they are
referring to you and I because we are a
personification of superb in every way.

Sir, you deserve the world, and it's me, I'm
your world.

I'd sell my soul to save your car from being
repossessed.
 because without your car what would you use
to drive me wild and crazy.
If this is a love potion making me sound crazy,
then add more of it because for you I don't
mind losing every ounce of my brain.

I TRIED

The song you introduced to me still plays in my
head on repeat like a broken record.
I shed a tear whenever it plays on the radio
because it resurfaces our memories.
 Yet sometimes it puts a smile on my face.

so, I guess it gives me Mixed emotions,
Just like you.

Tell me where I went wrong.
Just yesterday I was your reason to live,
Today I am your bane of life.
Your sudden change of attitude made me hate
the idea of love.

Because of you I despise men.
Hearing a man say I love you makes me
woozy,
But I sleep with a clear conscience,
Because I gave it my all, I gave you my all.

I don't have any what ifs because I gave with
all my might.

Yet none of it was enough to keep you.
You make me feel not enough.
You are the cause of my body aches.
Ironically you were my aches reliever.

I SIT IN THE MIRROR ALL DAY

I sit in the mirror all day,
Wondering what features to change,
So, I can be enough, for you.
I want to hear the words, "you are beautiful",
And believe them.
Believe that they are meant for me,
That they describe me.

But how will they ever mean anything to me,
When you make me feel like I'm not enough?
When you like other girls' pictures,
Who is the opposite of me.
When you stare at them with desire and
admiration.

Your wandering eye left me with a wondering
heart.
I always wonder if I was ever the girl you
wanted, or just the one who was available.
You have dug a deep hole in my heart,

Where self-security and self-love used to reside.
And for that, I will never forgive you.

YOU TOLD ME

You told me to find better.
That you weren't worthy of me.
But all I wanted was you.
All that was enough, was you.
Looking at you on its own satisfied me.
But you kept on insisting: I deserved better.

Every day you showed me why you weren't
worthy of me.
Why you didn't deserve me.
Yet I ignored the red flags: red became my
favourite colour.

I thought time was all you needed.
To learn how to treat me right.
You once told me; good things take time.

Shame on me. Shame on me,
 for being desperate that I didn't know my
worth.

Yet you told me.
That we have a thing and aren't in a
relationship.

And so, I thought, I'd love you into loving me.
Yet you told me, to be grateful for the bare
minimum you were giving me,
That you were doing me a Favor by giving me
your time.
Because being with you is a blessing.
And I thought you were right.
I thought that was all you were capable of.

But for her you did all I ever asked for.
It killed me to realize, you were capable,
But chose not to.
You could've treated me better,
You had it in you.
You just didn't want to.

You told me you wouldn't put any effort in us,
Because I'd do it on your behalf.
And I did.

You'd occasionally tell me; you don't want me.
I'd laugh it off.
But you meant every letter.
It is now I realize: You never loved me.

IS IT WORTH IT?

There is no greater feeling than that of love.
The butterflies in your stomach when he texts
you,
Or when they mention his name.
The adoration when you think of him,
Finding yourself smiling.

But.
No feeling is as agonizing as that of a breakup.
That whenever you think about it,
Your heart starts beating faster.
As though there is a horse racing competition
hosted in your chest.

Yes, being in love is blissful.
But what about fate?
Inevitably you will be alone,
Just as you were in the womb.

So, whenever I'm in love, I fail to overlook the
mere fact that it'll leave me broken.
So instead of living in the present,
I think about destiny.
Because eventually it will end.

Someone tells me if it's worth it.
Tell me it being in love is worth the sleepless
nights I'll be suffering from, when it ends.

Yes, being in love is heavenly.
But when it ends, it will be hell-like.
Because after all, all trips have a destination.

ALMOST IS NEVER ENOUGH

I am never out of words.

Expressing my thoughts through writing is my
passion.

So, they asked me.

They asked me to write about happiness.

About how beautiful life can be.

To gloss about the sensation of blessedness.

But how do I sermonize about something I
know nothing of?

How do I tell others to seek for what I stand in
need of?

I have been crying out for this feeling.

If it was oxygen I would've suffocated a decade
ago.

For then, life was about playing in the field.

The only hurt I knew bruised knees by falling.

Betrayal of friends: them playing without me.

The only hurt from boys: them not wanted a girl
to play soccer with them.

I thought growing up would bring me
happiness.

But today growth is my enemy.
Attaining happiness is close to impossible.
In the meantime, the tranquillity of the sea
comes close to this feeling.
Still and all. Almost is never enough.

HATE MORE THAN LOVE

I gave you my all,
You gave yours to her.
I loved all of you,
You loved all of her.
You made me wish to be her.
You were running through my mind all day,
In yours she sat in peace.
All those times I was begging for your
attention; you were giving it to her on a buffet.

I hated her.
I was angry at her.
She had you. All of you.
How can she get of all you,
When I'd have to beg for a small portion of
you?

I was meant to hate you for stringing me along.
But I hated her.
I was meant to leave, to love myself.

But I loved you more.

Clearly, I hated myself,

For wanting someone who didn't want m

I'M SCARED.

I'm scared that one day all our efforts.

Getting to know each other will all be in vain.

That the promises we made

will be meaningless.

I'm scared that once again,

we will be strangers.

Only ones with memories.

That one day I'll go back to being lonely.

With every passing day

we are getting closer to our destination.

One day you'll stop loving me.

You'll look at another girl with those eyes,

The ones you promised to only use on me.

I'm scared that one day.

I'll stare at my phone for hours,

Waiting for your text,

While texting me is the last thing on your mind.
Because you found someone else, your new
honey bun.

IN YOUR BUSY SCHEDULES

Hour after hour I check my phone,
To see if you remembered me.
I jump at every notification,
Hoping you finally found a second to fit me in
your busy schedule.

But I must understand.
You are busy securing your future.
But why is my heart still aching when there's
no text from you?

Sometimes I want to share good news with
you, I call you,
I forgot; you are busy.
I had a bad day, I'm in need of consolation.
But you are busy.

I go through my darkest days alone.
I celebrate victories alone.

I alternatively start arguments,

So, I'd get your attention.

I make noise to turn your head around.

I want you to notice me, to see me.

I know you're unable to drop your

commitments so we could gaze into each

other's eyes all day.

But I also know, I need love.

I need your time.

To feel important.

To know that I am a part of the future you are

securing.

But in your busy schedule,

My heart is getting used of your absence.

I WAITED

Our nightly conversations were my solace.
We told each other about how we spent our
day.
In our night calls I found antidepressants.
Your attentive ear made me feel loved.

But now you're busy.
Too busy to ask about my day.
Or wish me a goodnight sleep.

You'd promise to take a second from work and
call me before you sleep: rekindle our habit.
And so, I waited.
For you to make time for me, to love me.
Tossing and turning from the late hours of the
day through the early hours of the next.

With every beep of my phone, I jumped.
I watched the sun fall and rise again,

Meanwhile you slept like a baby.

Yet I'd still wait every day, for you to remember me.

But you were busy. Too busy to love me.

YOUR TEARS SOOTHE MY SOUL

I gave you everything there was to give.
I would've killed for you.
Everyday I'd beg for your attention.
Not money or materialistic things.
Just for you to pay heed.

Feeling your skin rub again mine was heaven
for me.
Hearing you say, "I love you",
Was a treasure to me.

Yet I had to beg you to say those words.
I begged for your affection,
I cried out for your love.
Alternatively, I beseeched God to help me un
love you.

And just like he promised in his word he
answered my prayer.
In my eyes you became an unsightly creature.

Yet today your eyes are filled with tears,
Because you have realized that you lost a
peculiar God.

Seeing you shed tears massages my soul.
Your heartache brings pleasure to my inner
organs.
Today you're begging for my attention.
Baby, are you a firework?
Cause you are loud and annoying.

Not so long ago you were taciturn.
Silent about your love for me.
I was a secret convenience.
It is now you are ready to love me loudly.
Baby, I outgrew you.

I am thrilled and proud to be able to look at you
and feel nothing.
If loving you meant grief, hating you must
mean happiness.

Baby, you are my source of happiness.

Similarly to how you were my source of grief.

13th of OCTOBER

In Gregorian calendar, it is the international
day for disaster reduction.
In my calendar, it is the day I met the man of
my dreams.
In United states calendar, it is national
metastatic breast cancer day.
And in my calendar, it is the day I met the man
who made my heart feel at ease.
Who reminded me of sunsets and waterfalls.

Yet in the same calendar of mine,
It is the day I met the man who defined hurt for
me,
The man who promised me heaven and earth.
Yet delivered hell on a silver platter.
The man who led my heart to its grave.
who let me lay on his chest whilst another
woman resided deep in his heart.

In my calendar, it is the day a man sold my

dreams that he had no intentions to fulfil.

The day I stopped believing in love,

and the hope of ever falling in love again.

IF I DIE TOO SOON

If I leave too soon, know that I lived.
I didn't survive, i lived.
I didn't go with the flaw nor
swift wherever the world takes me.
I lived by my own will.
I made the rules. I did all i could.
My life was a success, in my eyes i won

TO THOSE

To those who are asking what they can do to
fix things after doing wrong to someone.

Maybe you should try putting their hearts
together like you would with a broken glass.
Try saying you're sorry to that milk you spilt
see if it goes back to the glass and all becomes
well.

Try sewing their mental health back together
like you would with a ripped pantyhose. Try
giving them the trust and security they had in
people before your betrayal.

See? Sorry doesn't fix everything. An apology
doesn't amend all wounds.

I survived

I believe now more than ever that nothing can phase me or drift me out of the way. Nor be my downfall.

I survived when no one knew i was going through the darkest phase of my life.

I managed to pull myself together everyday and show up.

I stood tall everyday and lived.